Darab dastur Peshotan Sanjana

The Position of Zoroastrian Women in Remote Antiquity

Darab dastur Peshotan Sanjana

The Position of Zoroastrian Women in Remote Antiquity

ISBN/EAN: 9783744679237

Printed in Europe, USA, Canada, Australia, Japan

Cover: Foto ©ninafisch / pixelio.de

More available books at **www.hansebooks.com**

THE

Position of Zoroastrian Women

IN

REMOTE ANTIQUITY,

AS ILLUSTRATED IN THE AVESTA,

THE SACRED BOOKS OF THE PARSEES.

BEING A LECTURE DELIVERED AT BOMBAY

On the 18th of April 1892,

BY

DARAB DASTUR PESHOTAN SANJANA, B.A.

Bombay :
EDUCATION SOCIETY'S STEAM PRESS.

1892.

TO

The Memory

OF

Lady Avanbai Jamshedjee Jeejeebhai,

One of the Pious Founders of

The Sir Jamshedjee Jeejeebhai
Zarthoshti Madressa,

THE BEST INSTITUTION IN INDIA

For the Dissemination and Progress of
Religious Research

Among the Zoroastrian Community,

This Book is respectfully inscribed with grati-
tude for all that the Institution has
taught the Author,

DARAB D. P. SANJANA.

PREFACE.

Actuated by the reasons I have mentioned in pages 4—6 of this book, this Lecture on the " Position of Zoroastrian Women
in Remote Antiquity " was delivered by me
on the 18th of April, under the Presidency
of the Honourable Sir Raymond West,
G.C.I.E., LL.D. (Member of Council), in
the Bai Bhikaijee Shahpurjee Bengalee
Hall of the Parsee Girls' School at Bombay.
In it I have generally adhered to the
earliest fragments of the Zoroastrian literature, and collected most of the references
to my subject in the Sacred Writings of the
Parsees. It has been my object to show
the extent to which Zoroastrian men had,
in very olden times, cherished respect for
women, and the position they assigned to
them in social, moral and religious relations—a position if not nobler, at least
as noble as that accorded to them by the

most civilized nations known in the history of the world. The special attention of some European writers is humbly drawn to it, as they occasionally seem to be unfamiliar with the history and antiquity of Zoroastrian Iran.

As nearly half the cost of printing and publishing this discourse has been made up by the kind support of the Trustees of the Sir Jamshedjee Translation Fund and of a few other patrons of Zoroastrian research (I myself paying the remaining half,) this volume, like its predecessor on the alleged practice of " Next-of-kin Marriages in Old Iran ", is intended for gratuitous circulation amongst my Community, as well as for presentation to European Avesta scholars and to the principal libraries in India and Europe.

D. D. P. S.

10th May 1892.

CONTENTS.

POSITION OF ZOROASTRIAN WOMEN IN REMOTE ANTIQUITY.

Among the famous peoples of remote antiquity—be they Indo-Iranians or Indo-Europeans—there was no community in which man had more unselfish sympathy with woman than the Zoroastrian nation that lived in the Eastern territories of Iran more than three thousand years ago. Under the influence of monotheism, and by a close observation of the sublime powers of the Deity reflected in His work in Nature, the Zoroastrian man of ancient Iran had become naturally capable of appreciating the different blessings God had bestowed upon him by the creation of womankind. In primitive Iranian society the wife held a position, in social as well as spiritual relations, not inferior to her spouse, husband or lord. The wife, the mother, the daughter were beings for whom the husband, the son, the father had very anxious regard.

" When we are seeking," says Mr. Gladstone,
" to ascertain the measure of that conception
which any given race has formed of our nature,
there is, perhaps, no single test so effective as
the position which it assigns to women. For, as
the law of force is the law of the brute creation,
so, in proportion as he is under the yoke of that
law, does man approximate to the brute; and in
proportion, on the other hand, as he has escaped
from its dominion, is he ascending into the higher
sphere of being, and claiming relationship with
Deity." So the probable test of the ancient
Iranian civilization, lies in the social and moral
position which that nation assigned to its women.

Two important facts have persuaded me to
select for to-day's lecture the subject of the
social status of Zoroastrian women in ancient
Iran. First, the general system of training imparted to Parsee girls in Bombay, which has
lately been drawing to it very great attention.
I trust that a treatment of the theme I have
chosen, will remind us of our divergence in these
days from the system of moral and spiritual
culture which is so well emphasized in the
ancient Zoroastrian books as the useful factor in

the mental development of the female sex. Secondly, the common opinion of English writers on the history of civilization and morals, that the civilized nations of the East were, before the advent of Christianity into this world, quite unfamiliar with the highest and noblest ideas regarding woman which are embodied in the New Testament. Hence Christianity is supposed to be "the origin of many of the purest elements of our civilization." In the "History of the Rise and Influence of the spirit of Rationalism in Europe," by W. E. H. Lecky (Vol. I., page 213), we light upon this European or Christian standpoint: "Seldom or never has there been one which has exercised a more profound and, on the whole, a more salutary influence than the mediæval conception of the Virgin. For the first time woman was elevated to her rightful position, and the sanctity of weakness was recognized as well as the sanctity of sorrow . . . . . Into a harsh and ignorant and benighted age this ideal type infused a conception of gentleness and of purity unknown to the proudest civilizations of the past." How far Mr. Lecky's view is open to exceptions, may be easily observed by a cursory glance at the most ancient ideas regarding woman, which Zoroastrism had taught to mankind many centuries before the Christian doctrines came into existence.[1]

I have here generally confined myself to the existing fragments of the Zand-Avesta—a European designation very commonly applied to the Sacred Books of the Parsee community. The proper scientific name of the Parsee Scriptures is the *Avista*, *i. e.*, the Revelation of what is unknown, or, according to the Vedic *Avesta*, the book containing moral and ceremonial laws. The most ancient Avesta fragments now extant, form only about one-third of the original whole, comprehended in the twenty-one Nasks of the entire Avesta literature, the rest having been scattered or destroyed during foreign conquests. Though incomplete, these existing portions have enshrined a few materials which would enable us to form an

---

[1] Mr. Lilly says in his "Right and Wrong," p. 204: "Nowhere is the immeasurable superiority of Christianity to the rest of the world's creeds more clearly manifested than in its ideal and law of matrimony." Such opinions may be attributed to the ignorance of English philosophers of Zoroaster's ideal of women in the Parsee Scriptures, which was attained by the Zoroastrians in the more ancient Avesta period.

idea in outline of the training and organization
of the Zoroastrian family in the golden age of
the Zoroastrian people. These references have
been brought to light to a certain extent by
European and Parsee writers. Among the former
I may mention Spiegel, Geiger, Darmesteter,
Harlez, Casartelli and Zimmer; among the latter
the renowned historian, Mr. Dosabhai Framjee
Karaka, and Mr. Sohrabjee Shahpurjee Bengalee.[1] It is a happy coincidence that the liberal
donor of this magnificent building [2] and a pioneer
of Parsee female education, Mr. Sohrabjee Bengalee, was the first to attempt, more than 30
years ago, a special discourse upon the position

---

[1] As my authorities I may here mention Drs. West, Dar-
mesteter and Mills in Max Müller's "Sacred Books of the
East," Vols. IV., V., XVIII., XXIII., XXIV., XXXI.;—
Spiegel (Eranische Altertumskunde, Vol. III. ; and Arische
Periode) ;—Justi (Geschichte der orientalischen Völker im
Altertum) ;—Geiger (Ostiranische Kultur im Altertum) ;—
Schrader (Sprachvergleichung and Urgeschichte) ;—Rapp
(Die Religion und Sitte der Perser und übrigen Iranier nach
den griechischen and römischen Queller) ;—Westermarck
(History of Human Marriage) ;—Harlez (Livre sacré du
Zoroastrisme) ;—Casartelli (La Philosophie religieuse du
Mazdeisme sous les Sassanides) ; and Zimmer (Indisches
Leben).

[2] The Bai Bhikaiji Shahpurjee Bengalee Buildings of the
Parsee Girls' School, Bombay.

of Zoroastrian women in ancient Iran, in a contribution on this subject to a quarterly native journal, the *Jagat Premi*.

The time at my disposal will not permit me to submit a comparative treatment of the position of women in the Indo-Iranian period, a question which I hope to handle on a future occasion. My purpose has been simply to lay before you the general substance of primitive Zoroastrian thought on the training and position of women as illustrated in our most ancient writings. I have not on this occasion pointed to any of the references that are obscure or ambiguous; my humble observations have been restricted to the authority of lucid allusions and passages.

At the outset I may be allowed to say a word regarding the literary position of the Iranian people at the time when the illustrious movement, or the Revelation in Religion, was inaugurated by *Zarathushtra Spitama, i. e.*, Zoroaster. It issued as a monotheistic appeal to the free will of the different nations that then inhabited Central Asia, and had in view that noblest of all objects—progress and renovation—in the sphere of human thought concerning the power

of the Highest in the Universe. Previous to
that moral and spiritual movement, we ought to
assume the existence of a certain kind of pre-
development or preparation of ideas for its acceptance. No doubt the Iranian nation had become
fully sensible in the Avesta period of the want
of some powerful spiritual help, and its talents
were capable of reasoning upon Zoroaster's doctrines and of discovering the truth embodied in
them. Under such circumstances we can readily
believe that the Zoroastrian nation, in the age of
the Avesta, was composed of men and women who
had already been brought up amidst civilized
surroundings. The philosophical sermons addressed by Zoroaster to both the sexes, in the
rhythmical style of the Gathas, furnish us with
a proof of the existence of talented women in
that golden age of Zoroastrian sovereignty. (Yas.
XXX. 1-2 and 9).

With these preliminary remarks, I pass onward
to the main part of my lecture which includes
(1), the subject of birth, training and functions
of the daughter of a Zoroastrian up to the age of
puberty; (2), the Avesta ideas on the marriage
tie; (3), an insight into the social and spiritual

status of the Zoroastrian wife; and (4), the question whether polygamy or monogamy was practised in the Avesta period.

The ancient Iranians had other and far higher purposes in marriages than the mere begetting of children. These purposes were not of a selfish kind. They were based or concentrated in the revealed hope of the spiritual elevation of the good creation in the end. The Zoroastrian faith aspires to a high state of spiritual progress which is to be consummated about the time of the resurrection, when the spirit of man will reach its purest or angelic stage. Humanity, according to Zoroaster, is born to fight out its struggle against evil in this world, and to adhere to and strengthen the cause of good. The principal impetus to a marriage conclusion is, consequently, the desire to contribute to the great renovation hereafter, which is promised for humanity. This renovation cannot be carried out in the individual self, but must be gradually worked out through a continuous line of sons, grandsons, and great-grandsons. The motive of marriage for the Iranians was, therefore, sacred. It was a religious purpose which they had in view when the male and female individuals contributed by marital union (*nâirithwana*) their assistance (1), in the propagation of the human race; (2), in spreading the Zoroastrian faith; and (3), in giving stability to the religious kingdom of God by contributing to the victory of the good cause—which victory will be complete about the time of the resurrection.[1] (Yasna LXVIII. 5; XXX. 9; XXXIV· 15; XLVI. 3; LXX. 5; Yasht XIX. 89, 98; VIII. 15; X. 38, 65; XIII. 148-155).

The objects of the marriage bond were, therefore, purely religious, tending to the success of light, piety or virtue in this world. For this reason the old Iranian honours " the mother of many children, of many sons, of many bold talented sons." (*Vide* Visp. I. 5, etc.) The Greek historians say that a mother received from the king valuable awards for her helpful

---

[1] According to Becker's *Charicles* (pp. 475 *seq.*) " There were three considerations by which the duty of marriage was enforced among the ancient Greeks : I. Respect to the gods; for it was incumbent on every one to leave behind him those who should continue to discharge his religious obligations. II. Obligation to the State ; since by generating descendants, its continuance was provided for. III. A regard for their own race and lineage to discharge the duties to the departed."

hand in the increase of the race.[1] "Male children," "a troop of male children," and "the purity of one's soul," are blessings of equal merit in the Avesta (Yt. VIII. 15.)[2] The gift of sons is as good as the gift of a sovereignty, or of bliss in heaven. (Yt. X. 65.) Bright children and a direct line of descendants, are bestowed upon pious women by Haoma. (Yas. IX. 22.) Hence the Avesta declares that "the married man is far above him who is unmarried; he who has a settled home is far above him who has none; he who has children is far above him who has no offspring."—(Vend. IV. 47.) One of the benedictions which Zoroaster pronounced upon

---

[1] Cf. Fr. Spiegel. "Nach Strabo (XV. 733) setzte der König Belohnungen für diejenigen aus, welche die meisten Söhne erzeugt hatten." (Vol. III., p. 681.)

[2] Compare the *Manusmriti*, or the Institutes of the Sacred Law proclaimed by Manu (S. B. E., Vol. XXV., Chap. IX., 26-28) :—" Between wives who (are destined) to bear children, who secure many blessings, who are worthy of worship and irradiate (their) dwellings, and between the goddesses of fortune, (who reside,) in the houses (of men), there is no difference whatever. The production of children, the nurture of those born, and the daily life of men, (of these matters) woman is visibly the cause. Offspring, (the due performance of,) religious rites, faithful service, highest conjugal happiness and heavenly bliss for the ancestors and oneself depend on one's wife alone."

King Vishtâspa is : "May you (*i.e.*, King Vishtâspa and Queen Hutaosa) procreate ten male
offspring resembling yourselves in their bodily
constitution ! May three of them follow the voca-
tion of the priest, three the tactics of the warrior,
and three agriculture ! May one of them follow
the ways of Jamasp (*i.e.*, turn out a sage) that
you may be assisted with his most felicitous wisdom
for ever and ever." (Yasht Frag. XXIV. 3.)

[According to Westermarck, the Hebrews
have a proverb that "he who has no wife is no
man." According to Manu, "marriage is the
twelfth *Sanskára*, and hence a religious duty
incumbent upon all" (II. 66). "Until he finds
a wife," says the Brahmadharma, "a man is only
half of a whole." In ancient Greece, marriage
was one of the public duties of the citizen. The
old unmarried men or women, and even those
that married too late were, in Sparta, prosecuted
and punished (Müller, Vol. II., p. 300). According to Plato, "every individual is bound to
provide for a continuance of representatives to
succeed himself as ministers of the Divinity."
(*Nepos* VI., p. 773.) To the Roman citizen the
blessing of children was the principal motive of

life. Cicero's treatise "De Legibus" states that the Roman law imposed a tax upon unmarried men. "Children," says Hobbes, "are a man's power and his honour!" (*Vide* Bain, *Morals*, p. 142.) Josephus and Zimmer record about the prehistoric Semites and the Indo-Iranians, that they were very desirous of begetting sons, specially from the religious conviction that the departed spirits of their family would be rendered happy and gratified by the ceremonial homage and remembrance offered to them in the future by their male successors. (*Vide* Westermarck, pp. 141-143 and 379.) Dr. Oldenberg (in *Buddha, seine Leben, seine Lehre, seine Gemeinde*,) speaks of the fundamental duties of monastic life prescribed by *Buddha:* "The monk who has sexual intercourse, is no longer a monk; he is no disciple of the son of the Sakya house." (p. 350.) Celibacy was, in Manu, enjoined on young priests and on old men; but "the Buddha," says Sir Monier-Williams, "enunciated that 'a wise man should avoid married life as if it were a burning pit of live coals'. . . Buddha's anti-matrimonial doctrines did excite opposition. The people murmured and said, 'He is come to bring childlessness amongst us, and widowhood and destruction of family life.'" (*Vide* Buddhism, p. 88.)]

According to the Avesta, married men or women who are impious, are not capable of begetting children. The good spirits imprecate childlessness upon them.—(Yas. XI. 3.) This dictum of the Avesta is in harmony with the teachings of Nature, which warn us to avoid intemperate or impious habits, as these generally deteriorate the natural powers of procreation with which the sexes are endowed. [According to Westermarck, it is a Japanese proverb that, "'Honest people have many children;' the Chinese regard a large family of sons as a mark of the Divine favour; one of the chief blessings that Moses in the name of God promised the Israelites, was a numerous progeny; and the ancient Romans regarded the procreation of legitimate children as the real end of marriage."]

Among the Iranians in the age of the Avesta daughters were not disliked.[1] Although they

---

[1] Comp. Ward's "Views on the Hindoos," Vol. I., page 452:—"The Shastras declare that the daughters of Brahmans, till they are eight years old, are objects of worship,

were less useful than sons in the extension of the father's race, still they, too, were objects of love and tenderness, tending to help the Zoroastrian race towards the religious object mentioned above. There is no reference in the Avesta which exhibits any trace of the displeasure of parents on the birth of a daughter. On the other hand, the name *kanya* radically points to an idea of great parental fondness for her. [According to Manu, one's daughter must be considered as 'the highest object of tenderness.' (IV. 185.)]

The Zoroastrian daughter was reared on the mother's breast to preserve the purity of her blood. She was fed on milk diet for the first two years. The preliminary instruction seems to have been given by the mother herself. No

---

as forms of the goddess Bhagvatee ; and some persons worship these girls daily. The worshipper, taking the daughter of some neighbouring Brahman, and placing her on a seat, performs the ceremonies of worship; in which he presents to her flowers, paint, water, garlands, incense, and, if a rich man, offerings of cloth and ornaments. He closes the whole by prostrating himself before the girl. At the worship of some of the female deities, also, the daughters of Brahmans have divine honours paid to them. The wives of Brahmans are also worshipped occasionally as an act of great merit."

regular instruction was imparted up to the age of seven years. It has been remarked that " sin does not touch the child up to seven years of age."—(*Din.* Vol. IV., p. 263.) It was, therefore, incumbent upon the parents not to invest the daughter with the *Sudrah* and *Kusti*, before she was seven years old. About this time the daughter entered into the *airpatastân*, a religious school where she was initiated into the catechetical elements of her parental faith. The elementary religious books formed the sum-total of her school education. To make her qualified for her domestic duties, was a function that devolved almost entirely upon the mother.

When past the seventh year the boy or the girl was supposed to have become capable of distinguishing between good and evil, right and wrong. The investiture of the sacred badges after seven years, entailed upon the girl a due discharge of her common religious duties as a Zoroastrian. The Avesta as well as the Pahlavi contain indirect or distant allusions to the condition of a maiden in her father's home. General training in moral and religious precepts, the elementary rules of sanitation (Vend. VII., 60—72),

2

the art of tending domestic animals (Yas. XXIII. 3), of spinning and weaving the sacred girdle as well as garments (Vend. V. 67; *charáiti*, Yt. V. 87), of superintending the labourers in the field (Yas. LXVIII. 12) and the milking of the cows (Av. *dughdhar*), formed, as it seems, the principal acquirements useful to the maiden.[1]

---

[1] "Mr. Lane remarks that, in Egypt, at the age of five or six years, the children become of use to tend the flocks and herds; and at a more advanced age, until they marry, they assist their fathers in the operations of agriculture." (Westermarck, p. 380.)

Comp. Gladstone: "The Religion of the Homeric Age," p. 512:—"Of agricultural operations, we find women sharing only in the lighter labours of the vintage; or perhaps acting as shepherdesses. The men plough, sow, reap, tend cattle and live-stock generally; they hunt and they fish; and they carry to the farm the manure that is accumulated about the house; within doors, the women seem to have the whole duty in their hands, except the preparation of firewood and of animal food. The men kill, cut up, dress and carve the animals that are to be eaten. The women, on the other hand, spin, weave, wash the clothes, clean the house, grind the corn, bake the bread and serve it, with all the vegetable or mixed food, or what may be called made dishes."

We are told by Suetonius (Octavius, p. 64), that "the daughters and grand-daughters of Augustus were compelled to weave and spin, and that the Emperor usually wore no other garments but those made by the hands of his wife and sister." (Letourneau, p. 199.)

In public as in private home-life, she enjoyed the liberty of displaying her accomplishments. She was by her home training qualified to perform her household duties and to take part in domestic and public ceremonies; in short, she aspired to be the delight of her husband in the future. (Vendidâd III. 3.) On her mind were impressed the principal moral and religious tenets of the Avesta. She ought to be liberal, truth-speaking, God-worshipping, kind towards everyone, thankful to God, righteous, contented, obedient to her lord or husband, faithful and industrious, pious in mind, word and deed; she ought to keep her promises, to contract no debts, to remember and revere the dear departed.

The Zoroastrian wife was capable of attaining to the best virtues acquired by pious men. " We honour the pious lady who is straightforward in her mind, speech and action, who is worthy of respect for her accomplished education (*húsh-hám-sástám*), who is obedient to her husband, who is chaste and as devoted to her guardian (*i.e.*, parents) as *Ármaiti* and other female angels are devoted (to the Deity)." (*Vide* Gâh. IV. 9 ;

S. B. E., Vol. XXXI., p. 386.)[1] " She (*i.e.*, the maiden) shall be with a mind absorbed in piety, with words all directing to piety, with deeds all conducive to piety." (Yt. XI. 4.) So the Zoroastrian girl throughout her education was trained up and qualified for all domestic requirements in her father's house, at the same time her mind was steadily cultivated in the rudimentary principles of justice, righteousness and truth, just as in modern times children receive the rudiments of grammar. In the list of personages immortalized in the pages of the Avesta, for their sanctity, wisdom, heroism or patriotism, we observe a record of illustrious maidens. The 141 st. section of the *Farvardin Yasht* perpetuate the " holy maids *Vadhût, Jaghrûdh, Franghâdh, Urúdhayant, Paésanghanu, Hvaredhi, Huchithra, Kanuka,*" and "the holy virgins *Srútatfedhri, Vanghu-fedhri,* and *Eredat-fedhri.*"—(Yt. XIII. 141). We do not know any details regarding the good acts which these maidens

---

[1] Cf. Manu, IX. 29 :—" She who, controlling her thoughts, speech and acts, violates not her duty towards her lord, dwells with him (after death) in heaven, and in this world is called by the virtuous a faithful wife."

individually achieved in a cougenial sphere, but from the fact of their names having been handed down to posterity, and recited in public rituals, with those of *Zarathushtra, Frashaostra, Jamaspa, Maidhyômaungha, Uzava, Husrava*, etc., we are doubtless authorized to assume that even in remote antiquity Zoroastrian maidens had exerted themselves, with success, in rendering their names immortal in this life, and their spirits happy in the next world. [1]

---

[1] The following description of the chivalrous feats of an Iranian maiden, in pre-Zoroastrian time, will be of some interest. *Vide* Zimmern, *Firduasi*, pp. 138-141.

"Now the guardian of the White Castle, the fortress wherein Iran put its trust, was named Hujir, and there lived with him Gustahem the Brave, but he was grown old and could aid no longer save with his counsels. And there abode also his daughter Gurdafrid, a warlike maid, firm in the saddle and practised in the fight. . . . .

"But when those within the castle learned that their chief was bound, they raised great lamentation, and their fears were sore. And Gurdafrid, too, when she learned it, was grieved, but she was ashamed also for the fate of Hujir. So she took forth burnished mail and clad herself therein, and she hid her tresses under a helmet of Roum, and she mounted a steed of battle and came forth before the walls like to a warrior. And she uttered a cry of thunder, and flung it amid the ranks of Turan, and she defied the champions to come forth to single combat. And none came, for they

Hence Dr. Geiger says, "It would not be easy

'beheld her how she was strong, and they knew not that it was a woman, and they were afraid. But Sohrab, when he saw it, stepped forth and said—

"'I will accept thy challenge, and a second prize will fall into my hands.' (Because Sohrab had already defeated Hujir, and sent him captive unto Human.)

"Then he girded himself and made ready for the fight. And the maid, when she saw he was ready, rained arrows upon him with art, and they fell quick like hail, and whizzed about his head; and Sohrab, when he saw it, could not defend himself, and was angry and ashamed. Then he covered his head with his shield and ran at the maid. But she, when she saw him approach, dropped her bow and couched a lance, and thrust at Sohrab with vigour, and shook him mightily, and it wanted little, and she would have thrown him from his seat. And Sohrab was amazed, and his wrath knew no bounds. Then he ran at Gurdafrid with fury, and seized the reins of her steed, and caught her by the waist, and tore her armour, and threw her upon the ground. Yet ere he could raise his hand to strike her, she drew her sword and shivered his lance in twain, and leaped again upon her steed. And when she saw that the day was hers, she was weary of further combat, and she sped back unto the fortress. But Sohrab gave rein unto his horse, and followed after her in his great anger. And he caught her, and seized her, and tore the helmet from off her head, for he desired to look upon the face of the man who could withstand the son of Rustam. And lo! when he had done so, there rolled forth from the helmet coils of dusky hue, and Sohrab beheld it was a woman that had overcome him in the fight. And he was confounded. But when he had found speech he said—

"'If the daughters of Iran are like to thee, and go forth into battle, none can stand against this land.'"

to find a people that attained, under equal or similar historical conditions, to such a height of ethical knowledge." (*Vide* my Translation, Vol. I., p. 163.)—Hence Dr. Rapp is able to make the following observations : " The importance and value of this education appear, however, most clear by the cultivation of such qualities as magnanimity, the love of truth, justice and courage, whereby the Persian people have deservedly earned for themselves the name of a noble race. . . . The insight into the moral life was here evidently coupled with the cultivation of the religious belief professed by the Persians, which helped the development of morals through the fostering of virtues, and which system of education served to mould the essential character of the individual man." (*Vide* Mr. K. R. Kama's translation of Dr. Rapp's German work.) [1]

---

[1] Rev. J. Van den Gheyn remarks, "The Mazdian religion can boast of having the soundest, the sublimest, and the most rational system of morals among all the non-Christian religions. The basis of these morals rests on the free volition of man." (Essais, p. 231.)—*Vide* the same idea in Dr. Casartellié's French, p. 137, wherein the writer avers :— "La religion mazdéenne peut se vanter avec raison, parmi toutes les religions non-chrétiennes, d'avoir la moral la plus saine, la plus haute et la plus raisonnable."

Before her marriage the maiden was under the
guardianship of the paterfamilias, the grand-
father or the father, the natural brother or the
adopted son of the father. In her daily prayers
she frequently implores that she may have a husband, and attain to fidelity in the Zoroastrian
teachings :—" Grant us this blessing . . that we
may obtain a husband, young and of a beautiful
person, who will ever offer us good gifts, who
will live long and beget us offspring ; a good-
natured, learned and eloquent husband." (Yt.
XV. 40; cf. Vol. XXIII., p. 258.) "Unhappy is
the handsome maiden who has remained childless
and wants a good husband."—(Vend. III. 24.)

The ancient Iranian ideal of female beauty
consisted in white complexion, a tall symmetrical
body, thin waist, sharp eyes, and small slender
fingers. "Then approaches the handsome, physically strong and tall maiden." (Vend. XIX. 30 ;
cf. S. B. E., Vol. IV., p. 213.) The *Hadôkht
Nask* delineates " a beautiful maiden, brilliant,
white-armed, strong, well grown, high statured,
tall, with prominent breasts, straight, noble,
with a dazzling face, of fifteen years."—(Cf.
Haug, Chap. II. 22, p. 311.) The female genius
Ardvî wore " square golden ear-rings, a golden

necklace around her beautiful neck, and girded her waist tightly." (Yt. V. 127; *vide* S. B. E., Vol. XXIII., p. 83.) [1]

The fifteenth year was the normal age of puberty of the male as well as of the female. (Ys. IX. 5; Vend. XIV. 15; XVIII. 54.) At this age the parents or guardians of the maiden would endeavour to find a suitable match for her.[2] As the Avesta community was made up of

---

[1] Here it is interesting to notice parallel ideas regarding female beauty in an Indian book, the Sanskrit *Dasakumára-charitam*, by Dandin, which is believed to have been written about the end of the 11th century, A. D. The Adventures of Mitragupta records an ideal of beauty in pages 186-187, of Mr. Parab's edition, whereof I give the purport below :—

"This is just the wife to suit me; she is neither too tall nor too short, too stout or too thin; her limbs are rounded and well-knit; her back is straight; with a slight hollow; her shoulders are low; her arms plump and soft; the lines of her hands indicate good fortune; her fingers are long and slender; her nails are like polished gems; her neck is smooth and rounded as a slender shell; her bosom full and well-shaped; her face has a sweet expression; her lips are full and red; her chin small and compact; her cheeks plump; her eyebrow glossy black, gracefully curved, meeting in the middle; her eyes are long and languishing, very black and very white; her forehead, adorned by beautiful curls, resembles a piece of the moon; her ears are delicately formed, and well set off by the ear-rings; her hair is glossy black, brown at the ends—long, thick, and not too much curled." (*Vide* Jacob, pp. 268 *seq.*)

[2] According to Letourneau, "Marriages of children, especially of little girls, were the rule at Rome, since the nuptial

4

four distinct professions—the priest, the warrior, the agriculturist and the artisan (?), who held each his own respective rank, the parents or their representatives would naturally think of finding out a son-in-law from their own profession, or from one that was superior to their own, or one of a better lineage. The marrying maiden was, no doubt, very careful in selecting her husband, but she had sometimes to rely upon the judgment of her parents. Her choice was subject to confirmation by the latter. In very rare cases where the maiden had no proper guardian, she made a choice for herself. [1]

---

majority of the girls was fixed at twelve years. But they were often betrothed and even married before that age. Vipsania Agrippina, daughter of Agrippa and of Pomponia, was promised to Tiberius from her first year. The *Digest* authorized betrothal at the age of seven. In betrothing his daughter the father contracted a civil obligation, sanctioned at first by an action for damages, and later by infamy." (*Evolution of Marriage*, p. 198.)—" The young Greek girl could not dispose of her person any more than the Chinese or Hindoo woman could. She was married by her father." (p. 195.)

[1] In Manu, S. B. E., Vol. XXV., Chap. IX. 2-4 : "Day and night women must be kept in dependence by the males (of) their (families), and, if they attach themselves to sensual enjoyments, they must be kept under one's control. Her

The solicitations for the hand of a maiden were made through a wise and experienced friend, who served as an intermediary for bringing in the details regarding her genealogy, condition, and qualifications. It is to be observed that the ancient Iranian marriage tie was not the result of any capture or purchase, but of pure selection on the part of the marrying individual, male or

---

father protects (her) in childhood, her husband protects (her) in youth, and her son protects (her) in old age ; a woman is never fit for independence. Reprehensible is the father who gives not his daughter in marriage at the proper time ; reprehensible is the husband who approaches not (his wife in due season), and reprehensible is the son who does not protect his mother after her husband has died."—(IX. 88-92.) "To a distinguished, handsome suitor (of) equal (caste) should (a father) give his daughter in accordance with the prescribed rule, though she has not attained (the proper age). But the maiden, though marriageable, should rather stop in the father's house until death, than that he should ever give her to a man destitute of good qualities. Three years let a damsel wait, though she be marriageable, but after that time let her choose for herself a bridegroom of equal caste and rank. If being not given in marriage, she herself seeks a husband, she incurs no guilt, nor does he whom she weds. A maiden who chooses for herself, shall not take with her any ornaments, given by her father or her mother or her brothers ; if she carries them away, it will be theft."

female, subject to the confirmation of his or her parents or guardians. It is sufficiently clear that the maiden's choice did not fall upon riches or a man of money, but rather on a man of good lineage, of a good character, physically strong, talented, eloquent and religious.[1] As for the bachelor, the remarkable sayings of the Mînô-i-Kherad are as follows:—"Choose as your wife a woman, who possesses the accomplishments (*pavan gôhar*) befitting her, because that one is a blessing who is very much respected (in the community)."—(Chap. II. 30.) "A virtuous wife of a good behaviour aggrandizes conjugal happiness."—(XIV. 12.) "That wife is the worst with whom there is no possible enjoyment in this life."—(XXXIII. 14.) The sayings of Atrôpâta dictate to his son: "Love always a prudent and modest woman, and be married to such a one alone. Let your son-in-law be a man good-natured, healthy and well-experienced in his profession, never mind though he be poor."—(Cf. Dastur Peshotanji's edition.) From Vendidad II.

---

[1] Manu, IX. 14:—" Women do not care for beauty, nor is their attention fixed on age; (thinking) ' it is enough that he is a man,' they give themselves to the handsome and to the ugly."

we might assume a prohibition against marrying a lunatic, an indigent and an impotent person, an infidel or a leprous individual.

In the 14th chapter of the Vendidad, we meet with the following passage which alludes to marriage as a means of atonement :—

" As an expiation he (*i.e.*, a Zoroastrian) shall, with sincerity and pious feeling, give in marriage to a pious male (*i. e.*, a priest) a virgin, who has loved no man. . . ., a sister or a daughter, at the age of puberty, with ear-rings in her ears and past her fifteenth year."—(Cf. S. B. E., Vol. IV., p. 171.) [1] Though this commandment leads us to assume the existence of a belief that even it was a means of expiation, or a meritorious act, to persuade a pious virgin to marry a pious priest ; yet such marriage ties must have been formed rarely in a community where the exercise of free will (Ys. XXX. 1-2) was the principal factor under a Zoroastrian administration.

---

[1] Ward remarks that so great a disgrace is incurred by remaining unmarried that on one occasion a number of old Hindoo maids were married to an old *kulina* Brahman, as his friends were carrying him to the Ganges to die (*vide* Vol. III., p. 181).

The latest scientific research which has opened the secret mines of the Gathic or the most ancient Zoroastrian lore, enables us to prove the existence of a highly pure idea of an Iranian marriage. Dr. Geiger, in his German work *Ost-iranische Kultur*, makes the following observation (p. 242) :—

" Contrasted with the foregoing (*i.e.*, Vend. XIV. 15), a stanza in the Gâthâs, if rightly interpreted, appears to contain a higher and purer idea of marriage, and to regard it as an intimate union founded on love and piety. On the occasion of the celebration of a marriage, the priestly singer addresses, as I would believe, the young people with these words :—

(LIII. 5.)

ܣܝܡܣܣ. ܘܠܡ. ܣܪܪܕܟ. ܙܕܪܝܕ. ܘܠܝܐܠܢܕܝܢܢܢܡܝܢ.

ܡܝܡ. ܟܝ. ܝܐܟܕ. ܙܝܪܝܢܝ. ܠܐܝܢܝܢ. ܣܙܝܣܝܡ.

"Admonishing words I say unto the maidens, who will enter into marriage,

"And to you (the youth) I, who know it. Take them to heart;

"Learn to know through religion and of these (the parents), the life of a good mind;

"In piety you shall both seek to win the love of each other, only thus will it lead you to joy!"

The latest translation of these Avesta verses given by Dr. L. H. Mills in the 31st vol. of Max Müller's Sacred Books of the East, runs in the following manner :—

"Monitions for the marrying I speak to (you) maidens, to you, I who know them; and heed ye my (sayings): By these laws of the Faith which I utter, obtain ye the life of the Good Mind (on earth and in heaven). (And to you, bride and bridegroom), let each one the other in Righteousness cherish; thus alone unto each shall the home-life be happy."

The latter version is more in conformity with
the Pahlavi, and will be more intelligible if we
refer to the previous verse in the same Gatha.

(LIII. 3-4.)

"And him" (*i. e.*, the bridegroom, Jâmâspa)
"will they give thee, O Pouruchista, Haechat-
aspid and Spitâmi! Young (as thou art) of the

daughters of Zarathustra, him will he (*i.c.*, the bride's father) give thee as a help in the Good Mind's true service, of Asha's and Mazda's, as a protector and a guardian. Counsel well then (together), with the mind of Ârmaiti, most bounteous and pious; and act with just action." (The bride *Pouruchista* answers:) ."I will love and vie with him (*i. e.*, the bridegroom), since from (my) father he gained (me.)" (*Vide* Vol. XXXI. 191-192.)

These remarkable verses (3-5) of the 53rd Chapter of the Yasna or of the Gâthâ *Vahishtóishti* form a surviving remnant of the oldest marriage formulæ that were addressed, by the greatest of Iranian priests and poets, Zarathushtra Spitama, to the bride and the bridegroom, on the occasion of the marriage ceremony of his youngest daughter *Pouruchishta* ("full of wisdom") with the Iranian philosopher Jâmâspa.[1] These stanzas inculcate to us the oldest Iranian doctrine regarding the noble ends of a pious wedlock. The bridegroom, as it seems, is given

---

[1] See my lectures on the " Alleged Practice of Next-of-Kin Marriages in old Iran," delivered, in April 1887, before the B. B. Royal Asiatic Society, in the Society's Journal, No. XLVI., p. 134.

over to the bride to help her in the conscientious service of Piety, Righteousness (*Asha*), and Communion with the Deity. It is the duty of the two to love one another, with the mind of devotion (*Ármaiti*), with chastity and truth. The marital love was doubly strengthened by the lover's choice having been confirmed by their parents or guardians, so *Pouruchishta* the bride answers: "I will (now) love and vie with him (in love)." The fifth stanza impresses upon the minds of the assembly that it is the religious sentiment of devotion to the Deity which leads us to the path of love. Mutual connubial love is bred by a sincere devotion of the husband towards the wife, and conveys them to the enjoyment of the pure joys of a happy home.

These moral ideas relating to wedlock are also implied in the verbs *vadh*, *vaz* and *vah*, which commonly denote in Indo-Iranian dialects "to marry," "to have connubial relations." These verbs radically mean "to lead," "to convey." We do not know the nature of the ceremony by which the bride was led to the house of the bridegroom in the Avesta period, but it is interesting to find in the 85th *Sukta* of the tenth *Mandala* of the Rig-Veda, a figurative description of how the bride Suryâ was led to her husband's home. Therein we are told that it was in the chariot of the mind that Suryâ was driven, the bullocks yoked to it were the sun and the moon (*i. e.*, light or piety,) and the wheels were her ears. [1] Hence we might draw a parallel between the marital conception of the Vedic Indians and that of the Avestic Iranians. It was an instinct of pious love which drove the heart of a maiden to find her complement in the male sex and enter into the sacred bonds of marriage. [2] (Comp. Schrader, *Sprach verglei-chung*, Chap. on "Marriage.")

I now proceed to the social position of the wife among the primitive Zoroastrians. The common Avesta words which mean the wife are *ghenâ*, *nâiri* and *nmânô-pathni*. The first word means,

---

[1] In Becker's *Charicles* we find that the Grecian bride was "fetched away towards evening by the bridegroom in a carriage drawn by mules or oxen, and probably by horses." (p. 485.)

[2] We find interesting details of the Roman ceremony of conducting the bride to the home of the bridegroom in Prof. Becker's *Gallus* or Roman Scenes of the Time of Augustus. This writer observes that the ceremonious fetching of the bride from her parental house to that of the bridegroom, called

etymologically, " a begetter of children," "a bearer," or " a mother." The second is a simple feminine form of the word *nêrê*, "a male," "a man," " a hero." The third literally denotes 'the lady or mistress of the house' as the husband is generally called in the Avesta ' the lord or master of the house.' (Yt. V. 87; XV. 40.) Herein lies a

---

deductio, took place in all kinds of marriages. This ceremony regularly occurred in the evening, under the protection of Juno Domiduca, by torchlight and accompanied by relations and friends, amongst whom were women who conducted the bride to the *thalamus nuptialis*, and who were permitted to have been only once married. The bride having arrived at the house of the bridegroom festively adorned to receive her, ornamented the doorposts with *laneæ vittæ* and annointed them with *oleum*. Equally general was the custom of carrying the bride over the threshold in order to avoid the bad omen of stumbling with her foot on it. First, the bride saluted the bridegroom; the latter replied to this address of the former in an equally measured symbolical form. The bridegroom received the bride with water and fire, and presented these two elements to her touch. Next followed the religious solemnities under the direction of the Pontifex Maximus and the Flamen Dialis, in the presence of ten witnesses. The auspices were also taken. The joint-eating of bread by the newly married was necessary; also the joining together of hands by the priest. The newly married couple sat for a time on two chairs standing near to each other and covered by the same sheep-skin, signifying that, although the man and the woman occupied two different parts of the house, that they were nevertheless firmly bound by one common bond. At the celebration of the wedding a contract of marriage concerning the *dos* was entered into and sealed by those present as witnesses (see pp. 160 *seq.*).

liuguistic proof for the assumption that in the Avesta period the position of the Iranian wife was one of equality to that of her husband. A second argument may be alleged from the existence of the expression *pithê* for the wedded pair in Yt. X. 84 (comp. Ost. Kultur, p. 245; Spiegel's *Commentar*, Vol. II., pp. 566-567; C. de Harlez, *Av. tr.*, p. 236), which enables us to presume that the rights and interests of the husband and the wife were identical, and that the latter did not stand in the relation of a slave or a mere "bearer of children" to the former. In Yasna LXVIII. 12, the husband and the wife together pray to God and implore for help. Before submitting more important points concerning the high position the Zoroastrian wife enjoyed in ancient Iran, I would draw your attention to what foreign European writers have said on the authority of the earliest literature now extant. The latest German work that speaks upon it is the *Ostiranische Kultur im Altertum*, from which I translate the following passages :—

"It is characteristic, as bearing upon the legal and moral position of the wife in the old Iranian house, that she bears from the marriage-day the title of *nmānō-pathni,* 'the mistress of the house,' just as the husband is called *nmānō-paiti,* 'the master of the house.' The wife ranks thus more as the equal of the husband than his dependent. She is not his slave but his companion, entitled to all his privileges, sharing with him the direction and management of the household.

"In the Avesta both sexes appear constantly as possessing equal rights ; there is no difference as to their respective importance. Pious men and women are frequently named together. As in this world, so also in the next, they live together, enjoying in common the pleasures of Paradise. Wives are an honour to the house, and the good spirits, particularly Ahura Mazda, are represented as being in the company of female *Yazatas.*

"As in the Vedic antiquity, so also amongst the Avesta people, women took part even in the holy ceremonies and solemn offerings.[1] The ladies of the house who cherish good thoughts,

---

[1] Cf. Manu, IX. 96 :—" To be mothers were women created and to be fathers men ; religious rites, therefore, are ordained in the Veda to be performed by the husband together with the wife."

utter good words, and perform good actions, who are obedient and subject to their lords, are invited in the Vispered at the offering ceremony equally with pious and orthodox men. Further on it is said that both wife and husband naturally pray together, with uplifted hands, to Mithra for his protection and support. The following remarkable saying of the Rig-Veda is also in accordance with Iranian custom: 'Already from olden time the wife has attended the common sacrificial offerings and festive gatherings, she, the fosterer of the holy law.'"

This opinion, which is shared in by almost all Iranists, may be further confirmed by references to the Avesta statements that the Zoroastrian wife is capable of vieing with her husband in acquiring moral and spiritual virtues, and is a co-operator with him in helping forward the progress of humanity by ardent efforts to .suppress evil of every kind in this world.—(Yt. XIII. 154.) Wherever the Avesta alludes to pious males, it does not omit to make mention of females of like character. It speaks of a pious co-operation of the husband and the wife in the propitiation of God (Yasna. I., 16; XIV. 7, etc.), of just men and just women (Ys. VIII. 3; XVI. 9; LXXI. 10), of male and female saints. (Ys. V. 27; II., LVIII. 5.) The sixteenth Yasht records the earnest prayer of a Zoroastrian wife that she may not swerve for a moment from the Law of God. This represents to us that in her heart the lady sincerely wishes that she would be able to discharge her moral and religious duties amidst the material associations of this world. In the same section we are told that she worshipped "endowed with full knowledge" (*vithushi vohu-banghem*) of the ceremony. Again in Yasht XV. 36, the materfamilias seems to wish that her respect in the family would remain intact; that she would be loved, and respected by her husband, and become praiseworthy amongst her relations, (Cf., S. B. E., Vol. XXIII., p. 257).

Above all, we observe the poet Zoroaster praying in a rhythmical strain to the God Ahura Mazda, that the virtuous and noble Hutaosa, the wife of King Vishtáspa, may exert herself to assist him in propagating amongst her sex the moral and spiritual culture of which he was the great pioneer and teacher.—(Yt. IX. 26; XVII. 46.) [1]

---

[1] Hence Prof. Darmesteter remarks that "the moral victory of Zoroastrianism is the work of a woman, and that no picture of woman is nobler and higher than that which is drawn in the Avesta."

In the thirteenth Yasht we meet with a sacred
enumeration of wives and husbands whose names
are immortalized for their spontaneous efforts in
saving humanity from moral and physical depra-
vity. *Hvôvi, Frêni, Thriti, Pouruchista, Hutaosa,
Huma, Zairichi, Vîspataurvashi, Ushtavaiti,
Tushnâmaiti, Frêni* the wife of *Usenemah, Frêni*
the daughter-in-law of *Frâyazanta, Frêni* the
daughter-in-law of *Khshôiwrâspa, Frêni* the wife
of *Gayadhâsti, Asabani* the wife of *Pourudhâkh-
shti,* and *Ukhshyeinti* the wife of *Staotar-Vahish-
tahê-Ashyêhê* (139-140), are the illustrious names
that remind us of the golden age of Iranian history when women served with a pious motive as
preachers, warriors and patriots of their country.
In §§ 148, 149, and 154 the spirits of those
women are invoked who had fought all their
lives for the good of mankind, for the good cause
of that spiritual progress which Zoroastrianism
aims at. In a later Pahlavi treatise we find the
nine daughters of Spitama receiving precious
rewards from Iranian rulers as a recognition of
their help in the spiritual advancement of their
nation.

In the scanty fragments of the oldest Iranian literature we do not find a detailed picture of a famous woman ; but we can easily trace her work from the virtues and qualities for which right-eous women have been so frequently extolled.

The duties of a woman in the Avesta period were, therefore, not simply confined to the econo-mical functions of her household, but they had an important bearing upon the moral and spiritual progress of the Avesta nation. Her training had rendered her capable of serving not only as a moral teacher to her own children, but also to her own sex. What should we assume to be the result of the enjoyment of such a position by the Zoroastrian mother, wife, or daughter, more than three thousand years ago ?

Regarding the question whether polygamy or monogamy prevailed in Iran in the Avesta period, there is no direct passage which favours the one or the other. From some indirect references Prof. C. de Harlez briefly remarks : "La poly-gamie ne semble pas y avoir été admise" [1] (*vide*

---

[1] Relying upon the authority of de Harlez, the French translator of the Avesta, Ch. Letourneau says in his "Evolution of Marriage," London, 1891 (p. 150) :—" The polygamy of the monarchs of ancient Persia seems to have been copied from that of the kings of Egypt, or of the Incas of Peru. As for

p. 172); while Dr. Geiger says : 'Leider fehlt
es im Avesta wieder an positiven zeugnissen
sowohl nach der einen als auch nach der anderen
seite hin, und wir müssen uns demnach fast nur
mit indirekten beweisen und analogieschlüssen
behelfen. Söhne und frauen gelten als schmuck
eines hauses und die götter schenken sie dem
frommen in fülle. Hierin könnte man eine
andeutung sehen, nach welcher poligamie üblich
gewesen und eine grosse anzahl von frauen als
zeichen der wohlhabenheit und des himmlischen
segens betrachtet worden wäre.'—"Unfortu-
nately there is a lack of positive testimony as
much concerning the one as concerning the other,
and we must, therefore, content ourselves with
merely indirect proofs and conclusions drawn
from analogy. Sons and wives are esteemed as
an ornament to a house and the *yazatas* bestow
them upon the pious in abundance. This might

---

the Persians of more ancient times still, the Mazdians who
drew up the Sacred code of the Avesta, if we refer to the Zend
text, we find they had a most severe sexual morality. The
Avestic code condemns and punishes resort to prostitutes,
seduction, sexual extravagances, abortion, etc. Throughout
that portion of the Avesta, which has come down to us, there
is no recognition of polygamy, and the verses which mention
marriage have quite a monogamic meaning."

be construed as an indication that polygamy was customary, and a great number of women a mark of opulence and Divine blessing."—(V. p. 68 of my Translation, Vol. I.) My remark on this conclusion is that it is now as inadmissible as the rendering "abundance of women" (in Dr. Spiegel's German Translation of the Avesta) for the expression *frapithwo nâirika*, is inadmissible. The second word is the nominative singular feminine and refers to a single woman or the mistress of the house. The whole expression would rather mean "(where) the wife is well nourished or happy." Even if we were to regard the expression as meaning "many women or wives," still it would not imply the wives of a single man, but a number of married women living in the same house. Here I have to repeat what I have already stated in my note on page 68 of my English Translation :—Just as is the case in Parsee families in India, so also in the age of the Avesta we may conceive a Zoroastrian family as having married daughters, daughters-in-law, and even grand-daughters-in-law with the materfamilias at their head, all forming a group of more than a dozen women.—Even the very nature of the marriage ideas which are inculcated in the Gâthâs, and which I have just mentioned, does not authorize us to assume any trace of polygamy among nations that flourished amidst very civilized surroundings. [1]

It is possible that in later times associations with foreign nations, Mahomedans or Hindoos, might have introduced the practice of polygamy into the Zoroastrian community, but, so far as the Avesta period is concerned, there has been no mention of two wives belonging to one man nor any allusion even far-fetched to that practice. [2]

---

[1] " Where women have succeeded in obtaining some power over their husbands, or where the altruistic feelings of men have become refined enough to lead them to respect the feelings of those weaker than themselves, monogamy is generally considered the only proper form of marriage." (Wester., p. 500.)

[2] From the works of Greek writers Dr. Friedrich Spiegel makes the following deductions in the 3rd vol. of his German work, *Eranische Altertumskunde*, p. 377 *seq.*—In the time of Herodotus, Persians practised polygamy (Her. I. 135), and according to Strabo, the Median kings married many wives, and the Medians dwelling in the mountainous districts had no less than five wives (XI. 526). Polyandry was also not rare among them. Polygamy of the Iranians is supported by Ammianus, Agathias and the *Shahnâmah*.

Illegal union between the sexes was condemned as a mortal crime.—(Vend. XVIII. 62-65.) [1] A bad woman was unfit to offer any prayer.—(Yt. XVII. 54.) "Stand thou not near her, sit thou not by her side," is the exhortation to woman in Sec. 57 of the 17th Yasht. Infanticide was strictly prohibited.—(Vend. XV. 11-14; Yt. XXV. 29.) The destruction of the fruit of adultery in the womb, by means of drugs, was regarded as wilful murder, and was by law punishable as such. The sinful woman, her paramour and the procurer of drugs, were supposed to be equally guilty of killing the child. The illegitimate offspring ought to be fed and brought up at the expense of the male sinner, until it becomes seven years of age.—(Vend. XV. 45.) A sorceress is an accursed creature. Disobedience towards the husband is a shameful crime. Failure to preserve one's health in a lying-in state is also a sin.—(Vend. VII., &c.) A later Pahlavi book calls it a sin liable to hellish punishment if a mother fails to suckle her baby

---

[1] "Thou shouldst abstain from the wives of others," admonishes the *Minô-i-Khêrad*, "otherwise you will consume three things: the wealth, the body, and the soul at once."

or to feed it on her pure milk, or if she steals the property of her husband or disobeys her sovereign.[1] It is disgraceful if the husband fails to instruct his wife, and does not keep her away from doing evil acts (*Víráf*, Chaps. 87, 63, 99, 68).

My subject has now come to an end. The successful results of the system. of training imparted to the Zoroastrian wife and of her high position and work in the ancient Iranian community, may be easily marked in the moral growth and physical welfare of the nation under the sovereignty of the Zoroastrian monarch Vishtáspa (Gushtasp). "Let France have good mothers and she will have good sons," was a happy remark of the Emperor Napoleon. The literary attainments of the mother, her fitness to perform her household duties, her example of a moral and religious life, are more beneficial to posterity, to the future progress of a nation, than the impressions produced by the father. Moral and religious instruction ought, therefore, to

---

[1] Manu, IX. 13 :—" Drinking spirituous liquor, associating with wicked people, separation from the husband, rambling abroad, sleeping at unseasonable hours, and dwelling in other men's houses, are the six causes of the ruin of women."

form the chief element in the education of women of every country; for without religion there is no moral obligation, and without the sense of a moral obligation, no sympathy or unity with the family, race, or community.

————————

I beg to submit a few remarks which have been suggested to me by this humble attempt at discoursing upon the position of Zoroastrian women in remote antiquity. The first refers to the question: " Why did the lecturer omit to throw some light upon the alleged practice of next-of-kin marriages in ancient Iran, which had been emphasized by several European writers as the darkest shade in the picture of woman drawn in the Avesta ?" My answer to this is that the *pros* and *cons* regarding the alleged practice of consanguineous marriages among the Iranians of remote antiquity have been fully discussed by me in my papers on this subject, which I had the honour to read before the Bombay Branch of the Royal Asiatic Society in April 1887, under the presidency of the honourable chairman. The European standpoint rests upon a meaning of the Avesta word *Hvaetvadatha*, which, as has been shown by me, does not indicate " next-of-kin marriages," but " the spiritual communion of the husband and the wife with the Deity." It is a pleasure to notice scholars like Hubschmann, Geiger and Justi conceding that the Avesta contains no allusions to the alleged next-of-kin marriages among the ancient Iranians.

The second point I may be allowed to touch upon, is the absence of the brilliant ideas of marriage I have just quoted from the Gathas, in the marriage-formulæ recited in India. The present formulæ embody a double benediction in two different languages, *viz.*, Pazand and Sanskrit, including, about the end, three short citations from the Avesta *Yasna*, Chaps. LIX. 30-31, LIV. 1* and LXVIII. 11 I humbly submit that a lucid and rhythmical Gujerati version of the original Pazand be substituted for the present incorrect and often unmeaning Sanskrit

---

* Under the present circumstances a revision of the Pazand text is, of course, indispensable, for there is no meaning whatever in putting a question to the following effect, to the witness representing the party of the bridegroom :—"Have you promised to pay to the bride two thousand *dirhams* of pure white silver, 'and two *dinars* of bright gold of the city of *Nishâhpur*," when no such coins have ever been, or are current, in India. Every such witness confirming, as he does, this absurd promise in his evidence, becomes, from a legal stand-point, guilty of unconscious *mithró-druja* (perjury).

4

translation that is recited during the marriage-ceremony. It is highly desirable that some necessary insertions be made into the present formulæ of apt passages in the Gathas LIII. 2-5 that interpret very noble ideas regarding matrimony, and the mutual duties of the husband and the wife.

From the authority of the Avesta we learn that in the remotest Zoroastrian period the names of illustrious maidens, as well as of philanthropic women, were recorded or immortalized with those of eminent men. But since the Zoroastrian immigration into India, no such honour has been accorded to the Parsee ladies, who had, to a great extent, fulfilled the noble object of sympathizing with the difficulties of their co-religionists, and of helping forward their physical, educational and religious progress. We ought to hand down to posterity our respectful remembrance of the noblest deeds of Lady Avanbai Jamshedjee Jeejeebhai, and the charitable acts of Bai Mithibai Hormusji Wadia,* and Lady Sakarbai Dinshahjee Petit. Such a record of noble women will, I trust, tend to encourage female charity, and be conducive to the good of the suffering humanity.

---

* One of the eminent founders of the Hormusjee Wadia Âtash-Behram at Bombay.

SIR RAYMOND WEST'S OBSERVATIONS ON THE LECTURE.

[Extracted from the report of the " Times of India."]

If I am not trespassing upon your time, I should like to say something about the interesting address, and offer just a few of the many remarks it suggests in the way of comparison with other systems, and perhaps also some practical suggestions that may be derived from the most interesting picture of ancient Zoroastrian civilization, which the lecturer has so lucidly placed before us. *We find in the early writings of the Avesta, or of the Pehelvi literature—with which I cannot claim any acquaintance, but which the learned lecturer has so well and so deeply studied—a bright and a joyous picture of feminine activity in the early world,* which is repeated also in other early literatures—as, for instance, the Vedic literature, which is as interesting a subject to study for European scholars as is the Homeric and Hesiodic literature of Greece, and which present some striking resemblances. We find in it also a picture of the early world wherein had existed a much greater freedom and joy to the female sex than was the case at a later period, when wealth had accumulated and luxury had been increased, and when for certain classes women became more the objects of sensual delight. In the progress of organization and refinement amongst the ancient Greeks, we find that women, notwithstanding the extraordinary gifts of the people and their capacity to master most of the problems that interest mankind, were assigned a position which was immeasurably inferior to that assigned to them amongst the Romans. This had much to do with the different destinies of the two nations.

As was observed by me in another place on a former occasion, when the same lecturer gave a discourse on "The Alleged Next-of-kin Marriages among the Zoroastrians of Ancient Times," the Romans assigned their wives a very high place; they occupied an equal position, at any rate, in the household with the fathers and sons, although legally a father took his wife under his command and his dominion, both morally and socially. Livi and other historians speak of women as occupying an equal place with men, and in some instances they speak of their virtues and their capacity almost in the same strain as they speak of their heroes and their statesmen. But a remarkable change takes place afterwards, and that is to my mind the most interesting portion of the whole history of the position of women in ancient times.

Lawyers are well acquainted with the two common and sacred modes of marriage amongst the Romans, but there is a third mode, a characteristic of which is that a wife by absenting herself for three nights in the year retained complete freedom from marital control. The union of things divine and human between the spouses was thereby reduced almost to a mere dissoluble contract. The sense of sanctity was lost, and reparations came to be looked on as most ordinary events. Roman women, like other women, could not bear the strain of so great temptation. We find that, at a later period, in the time of the Roman Emperors, this led to dissoluteness and brazen-faced licentiousness, which probably had never been equalled in all history. I rather think that, no matter how accomplished the women may be, and whatever advantages they may derive from their independence and possession of property, and their capacity to rule their own interests, if they have no husband with authority in reserve, no dominating but kind hand to exercise control or command over their moral nature, they almost inevitably sink; and, their moral nature falling, the whole character of the nation they belong to, also share the degradation.

We know that Tacitus spoke half satirically in describing the Germans and the position he assigned to their women in his great work called the *Germania*. In extolling the Germans and the German women he reproached his own people. Yet there was a basis of reality, and women in the ideas of the Teutons were especially blessed by Heaven. This elevation of women brought about an elevation of the whole people, who in the end swallowed up the degenerate Romans.

The Teutonic race overflowed into Rome, but in the meantime a germ of a great revival was sown. Christianity made its influence felt in the Roman world, chiefly through women, who felt in its divine system, or the strength of its diffusive thought, a control and a support for which their erring and weary souls were longing amid the vain pleasures of thoughtless vice and dissipation, and ill-used independence. Out of the long night of decay sprang forth the institution of chivalry, and womanly thought in a fanciful way was once more worshipped. Much of the good, as also of the extravagancy of those ages, is due to the position assigned to the Holy Virgin in Christian worship, or at any rate in Christian reverence. This is another interesting phase in the history of women and women's influence in the world. Yet, side by side with this semi-mystic adoration of pure womanhood and motherhood, that pernicious spirit of asceticism was working, which has been the bane of Christianity. Happiness and joy became incidental, temptations were regarded as essentially sinful, and women, being looked on once more as a source of delight, were deemed ministers of evil. The baseness which misused their society and their fine sympathies, was ascribed to women. Their spiritual and intellectual capacities were put upon a far too low a level, and they suffered from it for centuries. Their education in any worthy sense was comparatively neglected, until the Renaissance with its outburst of new ideas and new desires, involved them in its great intellectual current, and brought them to their former relative position.

But the development, though great and fruitful, was yet in a measure one-sided: female education at that time followed very much the lines of male education, and actually in the fifteenth, sixteenth, and seventeeth centuries there were female professors, and very eminent ones too, at the Universities, especially in Italy. We observe, too, that amongst the women of rank of the sixteenth and seventeenth centuries many were scholars who could hold their own with a great many of the gentlemen who were turned out of the Universities. But what I wish to impress upon you is that this system, though apparently so brilliant in results, yet, after trial for a time, proved barren and unfruitful, and that because the right system had not been adopted. Under the new stimulus many exceptional women equalled or excelled many men, yet as a purely virile education was given, the mass dropped back from pedantry into frivolity.

No really effective discipline took the place of classical study, and except where religious enthusiasm illuminated the dormant faculties, the education of women became defective and conducive to a petty insignificant position.

After a long interval in England came the religious revival at the end of the last and the beginning of the present century, and by force of religion and their attachment to the position which religion had assigned to them, women once more laid hold on a true means of elevation and development. They felt a brand held out to them, a stay to lean on, a welcome voice of sternness commanding a pursuit of higher aims. Equality in this spiritual sphere was attained once more. Then came the moral and emotional instruction imparted by our mothers and grandmothers, from which their country has derived an inestimable good. All this ought to show us that there is something to be done besides instructing women in mere learning. Equality of education does not mean identity of education as between women and men. It means a recognition of some great differences and an equal unfolding of the gifts of each sex.

From the interesting paper read this evening, it appears that this matter was not overlooked by the ancient Iranians, who brought up a girl to fill a place which she was to occupy as a wife and mother. They did not make, or attempt to make, of her a rival with her father or her brother in riding a horse, or in drawing a bow—the special accomplishments of the Persians as described by historians—but they cultivated in her the qualities and accomplishments which would fit her for a particular station in life, which she was required to fill, and the distinctions as well as the agreements between the sexes. Thus the great value of a worthy human life was better fitted out, and each sex aiding each, a noble race sprung up. Such sketches as those placed before us by the learned lecturer must at once find a way to your inmost sympathies as relating to your own people, to those whose blood still flow in your veins. It has the element of reality, though perhaps highly toned, and, therefore, the picture placed before us by the learned lecturer, must have for all Parsees an inestimable value. It does not give any mere abstract view entertained by philosophers or scholars; it tells us what your race has done already, and what, therefore, it is certain your race can do again. We feel a sense of unity with our ancestors, and are drawn into an imitation not of any abstract ideal. There is something which is practical, and which we can determine to carry out to the benefit of ourselves and our people.

A woman's education, as one might gather from all this history, must in a measure be supplemental, or, if you will have it, complemental to the education of the man. Shakespeare, who has got something appropriate to say on most subjects, says of the bridegroom and the bride : ' He is the half part of a nobleman and she a fair divided excellence, whose fulness of perfection dwells in him.' Similar words, or even more eloquent, are also found in Tennyson's beautiful poem, 'The Princess,' which I recommend every Parsee lady to read and study. Women in a large degree have to fill a sphere of human life, which the male sex cannot fill up, and how they are to do it, is a matter which ought to be most carefully studied by all interested not only in the progress of the Parsee community, but in the progress of the human race. There is much yet to learn, the distinctive points have yet to be clearly made out. No complete theory of female education has been framed, still it is plain that noble-minded women, great yet feminine, were reared and trained amidst the ignorance and levity by which they were surrounded. I recommend, therefore, all interested in the subject to endeavour to see what method has been applied in these successful instances, and from that to deduce a theory . or a set of rules—practical rules—by which similar results may be obtained in other cases.

One thing is certain that greater attention must be paid to the moral and emotional, the imaginative and spiritual faculties in women than in men. Their intellectual development often depends on it, and all their gifts are mingled in a complexity very different from the standard male character to which male education is adapted. *Religious tenderness, admiration of high ideals, a love of self-sacrifice are all of comparatively easy development in well-disposed girls. A woman who has been thus brought up, becomes a centre of moral light, radiating noble sentiments and high feelings in the families which she is to rear and take care of in after life—a teacher of truths and principles treasured as sacred by her children, and linked in their memories for ever with all that has been hallowed and revered in the past.*

Thus, with knowledge and power in their hands, the fathers of the Parsee women, the fathers of the Indian women, and the fathers of the women of the whole British Empire, can make them the centres of enlightenment, and greater men and greater women will spring up, a crowning race of human kind mightier and nobler than any we have seen in the past. I trust that every portion of the society of this great Empire will resolve to take its part in so lofty an enterprise. I am certain if they do this they will supplement nobly and grandly that work, those functions of a University, which I have feebly striven quite recently to pourtray. These are works which should be carried on in parallel lines, with far-reaching faith, self-sacrifice and resolution, with a firm determination that in the accomplishment of that work none of those engaged in it, will prove unworthy or fall short of the duty to which he is called, in the station in which he is placed.

[Report of the Proceedings of the Meeting, extracted from the "Times of India," dated the 20th of April 1892.]

Mr. Darab Dastur Peshotan Sanjana, a well known Oriental Scholar, delivered a lecture on Monday afternoon, at the Bai Bhikaijee Shapoorjee Bengallee School, on "The Position of Zoroastrian Women in Remote Antiquity." There was a large and appreciative audience.*

* [There were present :—Sir Jamshedjee Jeejeebhai, Bart., C.S.I., Shams-ul-Ulama Dastur Dr. Peshotanjee Behramjee Sanjana, Dr. D. MacDonald, Rev. Mr. Scott, Messrs. Sorabjee Shapurjee Bengalee, C.I.E., Jamshedjee Nasarwanjee Tata, Kavasjee Kharshedjee Jamshedjee, Jamsedjee Bahmanjee Wadia, Jamshedjee Kharshedjee Jamshedjee, Jamshedjee Ardashir Wadia, Phirozshah Merwanjee Mehta, Kharshedjee Rustomjee Cama, Hormusjee Dadabhai, Shapurjee K. Sanjana (Barrister), Dr. and Miss J. Gerson da Cunha, Dr. Atmaram Pandurang, Khan Bahadur Cursetjee Manockjee Cursetjee, Miss Serene Manockjee Kharshedjee, Khan Bahadur and Mrs. Phiroze Hoshangjee Dastur, Khan Bahadur Kaikhushro Hormusjee Alpaiwala, Khan Bahadur Cavasjee Jamshedjee Lalkaka, Mr. and Mrs. Kavasjee Dadabhai Dubash, Mr. and Mrs. Nanabhai Nassarwanjee, Messrs. Jamshedjee Cursetjee Cama, Nassarwanjee Byramjee Secretary, Rustomjee P. Karkaria, Hormasjee Kuvarjee Sethna, Pestonjee Kuvarjee Sethna, Shehriarji Dadabhai Bharucha, Jivanjee Jamshedjee Modi, Darashah Ruttonjee Chichgar, Nanabhai Ratanjee Chichgar,

On the motion of Sir Jamsetjee Jeejeebhoy, Bart., C. S. I., seconded by Mr. Sorabjee S. Bengallee, C.I.E., the Hon'ble Sir Raymond West, G.C.I.E., LL.D., was called to the chair.

Having been briefly introduced by the Chairman, Mr. Darab proceeded to address the meeting. In the course of his remarks he said :—

(*Vide* Lecture on pages 1 to 50.)

Mr. Hormusjee Dadabhoy proposed a vote of thanks to Mr. Sanjana for the very able and interesting discourse which they had the pleasure of listening to that evening. It was, he said, as remarkable for the depth of research as for the conciseness of language in which it was expressed. The formulæ addressed to the bride and the bridegroom at the marriage of Porochist, afforded a beautiful example of the mental culture and refinement to which the Indo-Iranic nations had attained in the Avestic period stretching back to remote antiquity about three

Nanabhai Rustomjee Ranina, Fardunjee J. Parukh, Byramjee Nasarwanjee Seervai, Pallonjee Burjorjee Desai, Kharshedjee Maneckjee Kharshedjee, Mancherjee Eduljee Morris, Bahmanjee Jamsedjee Wadia, Hormusjee Jehangir, Bomonjee Byramjee Patel, Dady Homejee Dady Sett, Navroji C. Daji, Meherjibhai Pallonjee Madan, and several others.]

.thousand years before the Christian era. " Him will they give thee." As what or for what purpose ? " As a help." Not in the sense of helpmate only. "As a help in the true service of a good mind." The bride in the fulness of her heart and joy responded with a maiden delicacy and tenderness : " I will love him and vie with him in love." And mark the reverence paid to parents in that age : " I will love him because my father has ratified my choice." These exalted sentiments relating to connubial love, were not inculcated to the marrying couple now-a-days. He doubted whether any Teutonic race which had been always conspicuous for its veneration of the female sex, entertained loftier ideas of the marriage state than those embodied in the *Gathas* of Zoroaster,

"A perfect woman, nobly planned,
To warn, to comfort, and command."

These were not the vain effusions of a poet or recluse who had no concern in matters of everyday life. These sentiments had pervaded all classes, judging from the fragmentary character of Gathic writings. The most conclusive proof of the truth of this remark, was afforded by a cursory survey of the Persian Monarchy during the Sassanian epoch. It was an age of religious revival. The traces of the Macedonian conquest had well nigh been obliterated. The coins and engravings all pointed to a state of society not dissimilar to that of Christian nations in the West at the present day. Both sexes freely participated in the chase of beasts, in feasts and festivals, in sports and pastimes. In one respect the older nation was far in advance of modern times. Females were as capable of performing religious functions as men, and their efficacy was the same. The names of maidens and married women who had performed deeds of valour and patriotism, or accomplished the regeneration of their country by a life-long devotion, or propagated the Zoroastrian faith, were enrolled in, and recited with, the list of illustrious men. It would be a good thing if this ancient and wholesome custom were revived among the Parsees. It proves that socially, morally, and intellectually the sexes enjoyed equal rights and privileges. The discourse contained many topics worthy of a careful discussion, but he must stop there, as the honourable Chairman was expected to dwell

5

on the subject at some length, and who was better qualified to handle the matter, or with a greater affluence of illustrations, than he. (Loud applause.)

Mr. K. R. Cama, in seconding the proposition, spoke of the acquirements of the lecturer, who, he said, besides being a distinguished graduate of the Bombay University, had studied two European languages—French and German—and had mastered the various ancient languages, among them being the Pehelvi, Zend, and Sanskrit languages. (Applause.) Mr. Darab was like his distinguished father, who was the High Priest of the community, well-known for his aptitude for learning languages and profound scholarship. (Loud applause.) Speaking on the subject of infant-marriages, Mr. Cama said that he was much grieved to observe that a case of infant-marriage had been recently upheld in a court of law, and it behoved the Parsee community to make a stir in the matter and remodel the law which had been found deficient in that respect.

The motion of thanks was then put to the vote by Sir Raymond, and carried by acclamation.

Mr. P. M. Mehta then proposed a vote of thanks to the Chairman, and in doing so dwelt at some length on the eminent qualities which distinguished Sir Raymond on the Bench of the High Court, and his ability as a Jurist, and his long, disinterested, and most valuable services rendered to high class, or what was better known by the old-fashioned name of liberal education. (Loud applause.)

Khan Bahadur C. M. Cursetjee seconded the proposition, which was put to the vote by Mr. Mehta and carried amidst tremendous cheering.

Sir Raymond West, who was received with loud cheers, said that it was a pleasure to him on an occasion of that kind, which was probably the last on which he would address an audience of his fellow-subjects of Her Majesty born and bred in that country, to find his name associated with such sentiments as had been uttered by Mr. Mehta, and to find those sentiments so cordially accepted by the meeting. He felt deeply and sincerely how much he owed to the eloquent speaker who had proposed a vote of thanks to him in terms going so far beyond all he deserved. He assured the meeting that till the last moment of his life he would never forget the kindness shown to him, not only on that occasion, but on every occasion on which he associated himself in the cause of progress and the public good with the native community, but more especially with the enterprising and active-minded Parsee community, who were known for their sympathy and readiness for every good and noble work. (Applause.) He trusted that the ideas which he had just given expression to would remain a sweet memory with him and with those whom he would leave behind, and that the interchange of kind offices, a common interest in high and worthy associations, which, springing from feelings such as animated them to-day, would long do good, not only to this country, but to all parts of the world where the English race and the English language prevailed. It should be their ambition and their high point of sympathy to look always to some fair and noble future in which every element of a great Empire would be associated in the work of ameliorating humanity. (Loud applause.)

[Here follow Sir Raymond's remarks on the Lecture, which are printed on pp. 51-61.]

SYAVAKHSH AND SUDABEH.[1]

In the controversy which has up to now mustered the *pros* and *cons* with regard to my dissertation on the "Alleged Practice of Next-of-kin Marriages in Old Iran," it is a pleasure to notice how far European *savants* have been compelled to review the basis of their sweeping assertion that incest was a common practice in the life of the ancient Persian. It seems that a serious consideration of my arguments has caused a certain modification in the European standpoint. Impartial thought results in the plain confession that neither is incest [2] prescribed, nor are next-of-kin marriages recommended, by the Avesta. Greek authorities on the question are no longer quoted without caution. The only weapons that the dogmatist can find to wield against my position, seem to me to consist of such equivocal Pahlavi expressions as admit of more than one meaning, or of such passages

[1] A supplement to my lectures on the "Alleged Practice of Next-of-kin Marriages in Old Iran," delivered in April, 1887. See my contribution to the *Bombay Gazette*, dated 12th November, 1890.

[2] In the sense of marriages within proscribed degree of blood or family relationship.

in the *Shâh-Nâmah*, &c., as have no bearing
upon actual marriage ties, but only describe rare
immoral acts of a prince or princess.

In a recent number of the "Babylonian and
Oriental Record" we have been favoured with
notes on *Qaétvadatha*, by the well-known scholar
Dr. L. C. Casartelli of Manchester, with reference to Dr. Hubschmann's paper on this subject, "Ueber die persische Venwandtenheirath,"
published in the second number of the "Zeit-
schrift der deutschen morgenländischen Gesell-
schaft," Journal of the German Oriental Society.[1]
Notwithstanding his remark that "Dr. H.
Hubschmann entirely agrees with Darab that, as
far at least as the Avesta itself is concerned, the
Zend term 'qaetva-datha' has by no means been
proved to bear the meaning of incestuous marriage;—nay, that this interpretation is 'not even
probable' (this he proves at some length by an
examination of the passages wherein it occurs:)"
this learned doctor (Casartelli), on the authority
of Prof. Italo Pizzi, points to a certain episode in
the *Shâh-Nâmah*, and tries to prove that incest
did prevail in ancient Persia. It is, here, needless
to dwell at length upon this subject. It is only

---

[1] 1890.

necessary to consider what direct proofs can be drawn from Firdusi, the writer of that Persian epic. In the record above mentioned Dr. Casartelli's remarks run as follows :—

" Those again who are not acquainted with Prof. Italo Pizzi's interesting book on the ' Manners and Customs of the Heroic Age of Persia,' as preserved in the Poem of Firdusi, ("L'Epopea Persiana e la vita e i Costumi dei Tempi Eroici di Persia," Firenze, 1888), may be glad to see what light, in the opinion of the Italian Eranist, is cast upon the subject by national Persian tradition. Pizzi writes on p. 191—after stating the motives for marriages of near kindred, and quoting the Greek and other testimonies,—'Of these marriages among relations we have but few examples in Firdusi's ' Book of Kings.' But the traces of them, though rare, are sufficiently clear. Sudabeh, in fact, proposes to the young Siyavish marriage with one of her daughters. In that case the bride would have been a sister of Siyavish, at least on the father's side, as King Kavus was father of Siyavish and husband of Sudabeh. But Sudabeh went much further and proposed to Siyavish, with whom she was in love, that when old Kavus died, he might ask her for his wife and thus console his grief, which would have meant Siyavish's marrying his mother-in-law." [1]

The writer here does not refer to a single short extract, but to an extensive episode relating to Sudabeh and Syavakhsh, which runs over more than 500 couplets. (*Vide* "Le Livre des Rois," par A. Firdusi, publié, traduit et commenté par M. Jules Mohl, tome second, Paris, Imprimerie Royale 1842, pp. 208-230.)

Firdusi calls the prince Syavakhsh or Syavush. The name is identical with the Pahl. "Syavarsh" as well as the Avesta "Syavarshana," *lit.* 'the black man.' He is mentioned in the Avesta, in

---

[1] I here only touch upon this first reference, since it is to my mind worth noticing.—Dr. Casartelli says further on: "Moreover Rustem had married a sister of Ghev, by which he had a son Feramruz, whilst Ghev was the husband of Banu Gushasp, Rustem's daughter." In this remark there is evidently an error. Gev, Av. Gaevani, the son-in-law of Rustam, Pahl. "Rudastam," cannot be his wife's brother. I should ask the learned scholar to prove that Rustam was ever married to a daughter of Gudarz, the father of Gev. Gev, the son-in-law of Rustem, may be a cousin of Banu Aram.—As for the last allusion to King Behman, I refer my learned friend to my refutation of the question in pp. 36-38 of my "Next-of-kin Marriages in Old Iran."

Yashts IX. 18; XVII. 42; XIX. 77; and in the Afrin-i-Zarthusht, etc. He is the son of Kai-Kâus, Av. Kava Usa, the eldest son of Kavi Kavâta, and brother of Kavi Arshna and Kavi Pishina (Yt. XIII. 132; XIX. 71). Sudabeh, Av. "Sutavangha," whom Masoudi names "Soada," is the daughter of Shammar, King of Hamavar (see 'Barbier de Meynard,' II. 119), and wife of Kai-Kâus.

It is to be observed that Syavakhsh was not born of Sudabeh,[1] but that the latter was his stepmother, and daughter of the King of Hamavar, who had treacherously imprisoned Kai-Kâus, her husband, and often endeavoured to throw off his allegiance to that Iranian monarch. We should further consider the motive which would have actuated Sudabeh to propose incestuous union with her step-son, Syavakhsh, and also what sentiments were uttered by that prince when such an unnatural proposal was made to him. I would refer my readers to the literal French translation of the episode, which is contained in Mohl's second volume, pp. 208-230. For the purpose

---

[1] Compare Zimmern's "Heroic Tales Retold from Firdusi," pp. 172 seq.

of this paper the following passages from the free
English version of select extracts from the *Shâh-
Nâmah*, by Atkinson,[1] would be sufficient:—

"The history of the adventure of Kâus at
Hamaveran, and what the king and his warriors
endured in consequence of the treachery of the
father of Sudabeh, flashed upon his (Syavakhsh's)
mind.[2] He, therefore, was full of apprehension,

---

[1] "The Shah Nameh" of Firdusi, translated and abridged
in Prose and Verse, by J. Atkinson (London, 1886), pp. 146,
147.

[2] The original verses of the *Shâh-Nâmah*, in Mohl's edition,
Vol. II., pp. 220-224, run as follows :—

(١) من اينک به پيش تو استاده ام ۰۰

تن و جان روشن ترا داده ام ۰۰

زمن هرچه خواهی همی کام تو ۰۰

بر آيد نه پيچم سراز دام تو ۰۰

رخش تنگ بگرفت ويک بوسه داد ۰۰

همانا که از شرم نآورد ياد ۰۰

رخان سياوش چو گل شد زشرم ۰۰

بيآراست مژگان بخوناب گرم ۰۰

چنين گفت بادل که ازکار ديو ۰۰

مرا دور دارد کيوان خديو ۰۰

نه من با پدر بيوفائی کنم ۰۰

نه با اهرمن آشنائی کنم ۰۰

اگر سرد گويم بدين شوخ چشم ۰۰

بجوشد دلش گرم گردد زخشم ۰۰

(٢) بهانه چه داری که از مهر من ۰۰

به پيچی زبالا و از چهر من ۰۰

and breathed not a word in answer to her fondness. Sudabeh observing his silence and re-
luctance, threw away from herself the veil of
modesty.

"And said: 'O be my own, for I am thine,
and clasp me in thy arms!' And then she sprang
to the astonished boy, and eagerly kissed his

کہ تا من ترا دیدہ ام سودہ ام .:

خروشان و جوشان و آزردہ ام .:

ہمی روز روشن نہ بینم ز درد .:

بر آنم کہ خورشید شد لاجورد .:

کنون ہفت سال است تا مہر من .:

ہمی خون چکاند برین چہر من .:

یکی شاد کن در نہانی مرا .:

ببخشای روز جوانی مرا .:

فزون ز آنکہ دادت جہاندار شاہ .:

بیارایمت تاج و تخت و کلاہ .:

وگر سر بپیچی ز فرمان من .:

نیاید دلت سوی درمان من .:

کنم بر تو این پادشاہی تباہ .:

شود تیرہ بر روی تو ہور و ماہ .:

(3) سیاوش بدو گفت کہ ہرگز مباد .:

کہ از بہر دل من دہم سر بباد .:

چنین با پدر بیوفائی کنم .:

ز مردی و دانش جدائی کنم .:

تو بانوی شاہی و خورشید گاہ .:

سزد کز تو آید بدینسان گناہ .:

deep crimsoned cheek, which filled his soul with strange confusion. 'When the king is dead, O take me to thyself; see how I stand, body and soul devoted unto thee.' In his heart he said: 'This never can be : this is a demon's work— shall I be treacherous? What! to my own dear father? Never, never; I will not thus be tempted by the devil; yet must I not be cold to this wild woman, for fear of further folly.'

"On another day she sent for him, and exclaimed :—'I cannot now dissemble; since I saw thee I seem to be as dead—my heart all withered, seven years have passed in unrequited love— seven long, long years. O! be not still obdurate, but with the generous impulse of affection, Oh, bless my anxious spirit, or refusing, thy life will be in peril; thou shalt die!' 'Never,' replied the youth ; 'O, never, never; Oh, ask me not, for this can never be.' " [1]

---

[1] Relying on the authority of Prof. Mohl's French Translation of the *Shah-Námah*, Zimmern speaks about it as follows :—

" It came about that Sudaveh beheld the youth of Saiawush, and her eyes were filled with his beauty, and her soul burned after him, so she sent unto him a messenger and invited him to enter the house of the women. But he sent in answer words of excuse, for he trusted her not."

I have here to repeat what I have already emphasized in my lectures, that in this episode the positive refusal and repugnance of Syavakhsh to his step-mother's treacherous allurements, evidently prove that no such practice was in favour with the royal blood in the time of Kai-Kâus. Were incestuous marriages admissible, what possible reason would the prince have for describing the proposal as "a demon's work," as the act of a treacherous and wild woman? Further, it is to be remembered that the sincerity of Sudabeh's invitation is not beyond question. It is easy to surmise that if submitted to by the prince, it would have enabled Sudabeh to carry out her design for removing Syavakhsh, who was heir to the Iranian throne, but was not her own son. [1] The English translator further relates [2]:—

"Syavakhsh then rose to depart precipitately, but Sudabeh observing him, endeavoured to cling round him and arrest his flight. The endeavour, however, was fruitless; and finding at

---

[1] The first act of the prince on succeeding to the throne, would naturally be the banishment of Sudabeh, daughter of Shammar, the hereditary enemy of Iran.

[2] *Vide* p. 147 of Atkinson.

length her situation desperate, she determined
to turn the adventure into her own favour by
accusing Syavakhsh of an atrocious outrage on
her own person and virtue. She, accordingly,
tore her dress, screamed aloud, and rushed out of
her apartment to inform Kâus of the indignity
she had suffered."

Here, I believe, we light upon an interesting
element of political intrigue. There is the in-
sincere expression of maternal love on the part of
Sudabeh, the unwilling visit of Syavakhsh to her
palace (forced by the command of his father,
King Kai-Kâus), the unnatural solicitation of the
prince by his step-mother, the refusal of the former to accept her unlawful overtures, and, lastly,
the innocence of the prince and the perfidious
accusation against him by Sudabeh. An intrigue
with such an object not unknown in the political
history of ancient Persia, cannot lead us to
conclude that there was any natural or actual
proposal for the hand of the prince, or that such
a proposal would have passed without a meet
penalty as an offence against the throne. Even
granted that such a proposal were sincere, is there
the slightest ground for attempting to prove from

it the existence of marriages amongst the next-of-kin? Was any such marriage ever consummated between Syavakhsh and Sudabeh? When the solicitations of Sudabeh are plainly characterized by Syavakhs has a temptation of the devil, I am at a loss to see why my learned friend Dr. Casartelli should yearn to find in this story an important clue to incestuous marriages in old Iran.

There is another interesting allusion to the same episode. "Sudabeh proposes to the young Siyavish marriage with one of her daughters. In that case the bride would have been a sister of Siyavish......" It is surprising to find that European *savants*, notwithstanding their extensive knowledge of Oriental customs, have often failed to comprehend correctly the several forms of Oriental etiquette and address. I beg to submit that some Eastern terms for mother, daughter or sister, are not to be as strictly interpreted as such words are in Western languages. Those Europeans who have been accustomed to the Indian style of address, may have noticed that the Hindustani words "*ammâ*" or "*mâ*," and the Gujerati "*mâyaji*" do not literally denote " mother " in every case, but are generally used as expressions of address to any lady at the head of a household or to any elderly woman in the ordinary sense of the English "madam." So also the designations for sisters and daughters, are not used strictly in their literal sense, but they are a common form of address to ordinary young girls, female visitors, relations, cousins, &c. When, therefore, Sudabeh calls the young maidens of her palace her "daughters," it does not necessarily mean that they were her own actual offspring, but the term would be applicable to the daughters of relations, nobles, or other allied princes; and so any proposal for the hand of one of the so-called "daughters," does not in the least prove that the proposed bride was the offspring of Kai-Kâus.

I conclude this paper with general observations upon the reasons which have thrown some European Iranists into the palpable error of attributing the practice of next-of-kin marriages to the early Zoroastrians. It is a well-known fact that the *Shâh-Nâmah* is partly based on indigenous traditions preserved in the old Persian or Pahlavi literature extant in the time of Firdusi. The Pahlavi fragments of *Karnâmuk-i-*

Artukhshtar-i-Pâpak in (containing about 5,600 words, equal to thirty octavo pages), *Yâdgâr-i-Zarirân* (wrongly styled the *Pahlavi Shâh-Nâmah*, since it contains about 3,000 words, equal only to fifteen octavo pages—a short account of the war between Gushtasp and Arjasp), as well as the fourth book of the *Dinkard* (extending to about 4,000 words, and containing a description of the exploits of various Iranian monarchs from Gushtasp to Noshirvan), have lately been submitted to close research. These writings have furnished us with plain proofs that the epic of the *Shâh-Nâmah* and other genuine Persian books relating to the earliest period of Iranian monarchy, were neither myths nor fictions, but, to a certain extent, reliable works, the offspring of the earlier Pahlavi, which has not survived in its entirety. Hence it is not difficult to trace the error of the European view. We begin with the assertion that later Persian history is the outcome of its Pahlavi predecessor. For that reason I presume that ordinary Persian words for daughter, sister, or son, used in the first-mentioned, are synonymous with the words used in the original Pahlavi authorities.

6

Pahlavi is a composite language, containing the elements of two different root-languages, viz., Arian and Semitic. In it the words used to express the nearest blood relationships are generally Semitic. They are *akh* 'brother,' *akhtman* 'sister,' *benman* 'son,' and *bentman* 'daughter.' It is remarkable that in Pahlavi, as in Arabic and Hebrew, the word *akh* does not always strictly denote 'brother;' but in all these three languages it signifies 'a brother,' 'a kinsman,' or 'a friend' (see Richardson and Arnold). Similarly, Pahl. *akhtman* means 'a girl,' 'a sister,' or 'a female friend.' The Pahl. *bentman* denotes any intimate relation—'a boy,' 'a son,' 'a youth, or 'a descendant.' So also the Pahl. *bentman* signifies 'a girl,' 'a daughter' or 'a female kinsman.' It is, therefore, erroneous to restrict ourselves only to the meaning of 'sister' or 'daughter' whenever the Pahl. words *akhtman* or *bentman* occur.

'The genial and industrious scholar Dastur Darab Peshotan Sanjana favoured us yesterday with a contribution which supplements his paper on 'Next-of-kin Marriages in Ancient Iran,' which was read a year or two since before the Bombay Branch of the Royal Asiatic Society. Since that paper was read Madame Dieulafoy's striking romance of " Parysatis " has given wider currency to the received traditionary and historical belief on this subject. Madame Dieulafoy with all her pretensions to knowledge concerning Persian antiquities, takes Parysatis as she finds her in tradition, the consort of her brother Darius, and Artaxerxes wedded in succession to two of his nearest blood relations. Inquiry into the latest results of philosophical and ethnographic investigation would, however, have warned the gifted Frenchwoman against a too ready acceptance of conventional beliefs on this subject. We need not here reproduce either the earlier or the later of the Dastur's arguments on the subject. It is sufficient to say that he has gone far to establish the proposition that the Pehlvi terms, the use of which has led to a belief that next-of-kin marriages were common in early Iranian society, have a much wider meaning than has hitherto been attached to them. European Iranists seem to have come round of late to the conclusion, which the Bombay Dastur has set forth with so much industry and clearness—a result which must be regarded with gratification. For though, as George Eliot says, we cannot reform our ancestors, it is always satisfactory when we learn that they were better than they have been credited with being.'—[*Bombay Gazette, November* 13, 1890.]

'Mr. D. D. P. Sanjana handled an interesting subject the other day whilst discoursing on the position of woman amongst the Zoroastrians in the early times of the Avesta. From the rather meagre materials scattered up and down the Avesta, or the sacred writings of the Parsees at present extant, he has drawn a clear sketch, which goes far to show

that the position which the weaker sex occupied at that time
was a very honourable one—honourable to them as well as to
the sterner sex which conceded it. This position, it may be
observed, is quite the reverse of that degraded state into
which woman fell in nearly all Eastern countries in later
times, and from which she is perhaps destined never to rise
altogether. As was observed by the chairman, Sir Raymond
West, woman occupied a noble position in the dawn of civilization among several ancient nations, but as this civilization
advanced and nations became more refined, woman was thrust
into an inferior position, and she became the mere instru-
ment of man's pleasure and lust. In the dawn of Greek civilization, as preserved to us by the Homeric poems, woman
was regarded with great respect, and a great measure of
freedom was accorded to her. But when that dawn broke
into the bright day of Greek culture and the noon was
reached in the age of Pericles, the greatest blot in this culture was the degraded, almost slavish, state of their women
and their lax morality : by the side of Pericles stands Aspasia.
Looking to this country we find the same phenomenon. In
the earliest times of which there is any literary record, we
find that the Hindoo women occupied a far higher position
that in our times. Among the ancient Iranians, as Mr.
Sanjana has shown, woman was on the same level in most
things in her sphere as man. But in their later history, especially in the time of the Sassanides, when the Zoroastrian
faith became the state religion, woman, it appears, fell from
her high place and sank into a debased state. From Mr.
Sanjana's paper it is clear that the early Iranians recognised
fully the spiritual equality of woman with man—an equality
which, according to Mr. Lecky, was not recognised by the
proudest civilization of ancient times. Christianity was the
first to do that for her, and thus to lift her from the abyss
into which the Greek and later Roman civilization had thrown
her. But the Zoroastrian faith did it long before Christianity,
and may be said to have anticipated it in this its noblest

work. Thus this assertion of the spiritual equality of woman with man is one of the many points in which the Zoroastrian faith resembles the Christian. Another interesting fact brought out in the lecture is that the ancient Iranians paid great attention to the spiritual and moral development of their women, and in this matter their modern descendants should try to follow closely in their footsteps. For moral education, of great importance to both the sexes, is of peculiar importance to the female, and what is rightly called the weaker sex. Neglect of it, such as is observed at the present day in Europe, results in the disastrous effects which writers like Mr. Lilly have so vigorously exposed. And Parsees would do well to profit by this.'—[*Times of India, April* 22, 1892.]

' Mr. Darab Peshotan Sanjana's delineation of Zoroastrian women in remote antiquity shows research and illustrates his profound scholarship. He points out that in primitive Iranian society the wife held a position, in social as well spiritual matters, not inferior to that of her spouse. With an array of apt quotations to support his position, he con-cludes that the duties of a woman in the Avesta period were not confined to the economical functions of her household, but had an important bearing on the moral and spiritual progress of the Avesta nation. Her training had rendered her capable of serving, not only as a moral teacher to her own children, but also to her own sex. Illegal union between the sexes was condemned as a mortal crime. Infanticide was strictly prohibited, and disobedience towards the hus-band was a shameful crime. Sir Raymond West's speech on the occasion served the purpose of an exquisite frame to Mr. Sanjana's picture. Sir Raymond emphasized the point that there was something to be done, besides instructing women in mere learning. Equality of education does not mean indentity of education as between men and women. It means a recognition of some great differences and an equal unfolding of the gifts of each sex.'—[*Indian Spectator, April* 22, 1892.]

www.ingramcontent.com/pod-product-compliance
Lightning Source LLC
Chambersburg PA
CBHW022014050726
47499CB00007BA/2575